Plus Size Goddess - A Novelette

Cathy McGough

Stratford Living Publishing

Contents

"Magic is believing in yourself,

if you can do that,

you can make anything happen."

Wolfgang Von Goethe

To BFFS everywhere for all you do!

CHAPTER ONE

I NEARLY BOUGHT A new dress today. It was meant to be in celebration of reaching the next level of my weight-loss goal. My trainer had been right: increasing my exercise regime to one hour, six days a week had paid off.

As usual, once I was in the mall, the sweet scent of cinnabonn-y goodness floated toward me. I took in a deep calorie free breath, all the while imagining sinking my teeth into one. Just one bite would suffice. But no, I had worked way too hard to lose the weight — breathing it in would have to be enough today.

If you've ever been on a strict diet regime — working your butt off to get yourself into shape and healthy — then you'll know exactly what I'm talking about.

Goddess Creator Fashion was where I was heading. It was my favourite clothing store, a comfort zone for me. A place of refuge for a little over five years. Back then, it was the only store to offer fashionable clothing for larger young women.

To be honest, when I was at my biggest — size 20 — I hated shopping for clothes more than anything. Well, second to going to the gym or exercising that is. But this store, well, it made shopping for clothes a passion again. Before that, I was a frump. I knew it and everyone around me knew it — but no one actually said it to me. It was something I said to myself every day when I looked into the mirror though. I was tough on myself.

Then Goddess Creator Fashion came into my life. I found real blue jeans. T-shirts to cover my ass. Ankle boots. To say that I rediscovered fashion is not an underestimation at all. I didn't know what I was missing until I found Goddess. The place gave me back my confidence.

I admired a few outfits with accessories set up on display on the plus size mannequin models in the window. There was a cute black dress contrasted with a bright red scarf. I wouldn't have much occasion to wear it, since I worked in a call centre and the only people who saw me were my co-workers. Still, the Christmas Party was coming up in only a few months. I could definitely wear it then. Maybe I would knock someone dead, if not, at least I would impress myself.

I went inside and grabbed two sizes since I wasn't sure which size would fit me today. I hadn't treated myself to an outfit in months. It was always better psychologically to reach a goal before trying on new clothes. But I digress.

Once I was inside the change room, I put the dress on and felt the silky interior fabric brush against my bare skin. It felt good, smooth, and expensive. I checked myself out in the three-way mirror, turning this way and that to cover every angle — still something about it didn't feel right. It wasn't the colour, because the black looked elegant with my pale skin and long dark hair.

I stepped outside. Grabbed a pretty scarf with embroidered gold thread around the edges and draped it around my neck/shoulders. It helped somewhat, but still wasn't right. I found the red scarf, the one I'd seen on the dummy in the window and tried that out. Still, even though the dress was fabulous, and the scarf was fabulous — I did not feel fabulous. What the...?

Something about it was off. I tied my hair up, thinking it might help, to show a bit of neckline but that didn't work either. Perhaps it was too elegant for me?

I went out into the store and chose some jewelry in a final attempt to fix whatever was wrong. It still didn't do the trick, even though I loved the dress.

I examined myself in the full-length mirror from head to toe and it came to me what the problem was. Even though the dress was in a smaller size, it no longer suited me. The style, the fabric, the flow of the thing was for larger women. A scary thought occurred to me — in this dress I still looked fat. I still felt fat.

It made no sense. I'd worked my butt off literally and gone down a few sizes, but I was far from skinny. Everything in my closet was a Goddess Creator Fashion garment. Why this? Why now? I'd have to find a new store.

I needed a second opinion and so I went out into the main store area and looked around. It was busy and difficult to catch someone's eye, but in the end one of the clerks came over. She immediately began to gush about how fabulous I looked. She said the dress was totally me. Problem was, I didn't believe her either. Even when she asked me to do a twirl and the fabric swished. Even when total strangers, other shoppers came over and began to compliment me in the dress too. I thanked them and went back inside to change into my street clothes. I still thought it looked terrible, but in the back of my mind I wondered — what if they saw something in me I myself did not see?

I tidied up my hair and put on some lippy, still thinking about the dress. Before I lost weight receiving a compliment was as rare as receiving a black rose. I put on my socks and shoes... Nicholas Cage's girlfriend wanted a black rose before she would marry him, so he got one for her. Did you know they only grow in Turkey? Yes. So, you get my gist, black roses are rare like getting compliments when you're overweight. Having a black rose flown halfway across the world for you — now that's romantic!

I gathered my things together then made my way through the store. I carried the dress and placed it back where I found it. Ready to leave, someone grabbed my arm. It was the clerk.

She pulled the dress out of the display again and said, "It's absolutely you!" and then made her way toward the cash register.

I could feel my complexion lighting up like a Christmas tree. She continued gushing and I let her while I thought about how to get myself out of the situation. I considered turning tail and running.

"And it's the very last one in the store," she said as she scanned the dress.

"I don't want it," I blurted out.

"I already started ringing it in," she said with a pout as she continued folding it to fit into the Goddess Creator Fashion recyclable bag.

"Sorry, but I changed my mind," I said. In my head it was loud, but not in reality. When she moved in closer, I said, almost in a shout, "I — don't — want — it."

"But it's the last one! And I've already scanned it in!" she said so loudly I swear all the hangers in the store shook. She began folding the dress. She put it into the bag. She handed the bag to me.

I leaned in closer, as the other patrons began to move in to surround me in anticipation of a row.

My hand took the bag, before my head could stop it. I wondered if someone was filming us so they could put this up on YouTube. Everyone filmed everything nowadays. Other shoppers gathered around like we were a sideshow at a fair.

"Cancel it," I said. "Please."

There was a steep intake of breath from her for a second, like a balloon ready to blow. She tut-tutted like I had committed a crime.

I placed the dress onto the counter and took a step back, trod on someone's toes, they yelped. Mortified, I turned with full intent to run. At the exit I stopped again when a woman grabbed my arm.

CHAPTER TWO

S HE HELD ME FIRMLY in her grip, red talons pressing into my skin. Eye to eye now, I pulled my arm away from her. We stood, face to face. Toe to toe. We sized each other up.

She was tall and plus sized – no major surprise since it is a plus-sized store. She wore a black business suit, with a tailor-cut blazer. The blazer fit beautifully and combined with the tight pin-striped skirt accentuated her figure. She topped off her look with a blush of colour: a red scarf around her neck. Her long black hair with a fringe across her forehead framed her face very well. She was extremely stylish, even posh looking.

We laughed as she let my arm go.

"I'm sorry," she said. "I couldn't help but overhear your discussion a few moments ago with the sales representative."

"What of it?" I asked rather defensively — I figured she might be with the Fashion Police.

When she didn't answer, I became annoyed and took a step closer to the door. She followed me closely like a shadow. What the heck? Could they make me purchase a dress I didn't want or like just because I tried it on? Of course not. This was America and no one could force me to do anything. Right?

"It's just that..." She stopped and looked around. Like she was worried someone might be eavesdropping.

I took a deep breath, "Yes?"

"I'm the owner of Goddess Creator Fashion and I'd like to buy you a coffee," she said. This was a shock and I said nothing. "May I buy you a cup of coffee?"

It all seemed a bit suspect to me, so I still said nothing.

"I'd like a little chat," she said, "trust me it'll be well worth your while."

"Trying on clothes is thirsty work," I said smiling. It struck her funny bone and she let out an infectious roaring laugh, which bordered on a howl. I laughed at her laugh and we left the store.

My original impression was that she was probably a Size 12 or 14, but now, the way her jacket shook when she laughed, I figured maybe the suit had the slimming effect I had heard about on YouTube. This girl, a model, did a clip about how you can slim yourself down by choosing the right fabrics and cuts. This woman knew how to accentuate her figure.

Having nothing else to do and curious we left the store. Once we were out, she couldn't force me to buy anything.

We walked out into the mall and went down the escalator to a little café on the ground floor near the entrance. Although the place was full, the staff immediately found a table for us.

The host took us on a tour. We passed by the pastries, pies, and pavlovas. The chefs were busy baking in the back and the deliciousness wafted out toward us. When we reached our table, I fell into my seat, feeling like I had just consumed hundreds of calories.

Our server was there in seconds and the woman ordered a Chocolate Croissant gently warmed and a Café Latte. I ordered a Skinny Cappuccino and we waited for a few moments before our drinks arrived.

"You're a riot," she said as she sipped her drink and then made a face.

I couldn't think of an appropriate response, so I watched her pour one, two, three, four, five packets of sweetener into her drink. The sugar sat on the top like a mountain while she folded up each paper packet into small squares. When the sugar mountain sank, she stirred her coffee and took a long drink. Her croissant arrived shortly thereafter, and she began eating it with a knife and fork. It had been heated up and the chocolate centre oozed out all over the plate. She polished it off quickly and then used her finger to mop up the chocolate which she could not get with her fork.

I took a sip of my coffee as she ordered another Café Latte, this time Skinny. "You have to know when to stop," she said, smiling.

I nodded, feeling fidgety. My phone dinged on cue and I reached inside my bag and pulled it out. Just a message from Facebook saying someone was LIVE — Jamie Oliver. Couldn't watch him this time. I turned the volume off and began to pop it back into my bag.

"Have you ever done any modeling?" she blurted.

I dropped my Samsung onto the floor and its guts spilled out. I looked her straight in the eyes, to see if she was serious — she seemed serious — then I reached down, popped the battery back in and restarted my phone. I answered her question with a question of my own, "Are you kidding me?"

She took another sip of her Latte. "No, I'm not kidding."

"But you must be. Or are you mad?" Note to self: this is not the way to win friends or influence people.

"Why," she asked, followed by, "you are stunning."

In my head, I was flashing back to all the times as a little girl I pretended to be a model. I only did it behind closed doors, so no one knew. I was pudgy right from the time I popped out of my mother's womb. She had to have stitches, I heard that story over and over again. I used to steal my mom's high heels, dresses, and accessories. I would even spray a little of her perfume on and put makeup on too. Then I would create a pretend catwalk on my bed. I would stroll up and down the length of my single bed and my heels would wobble back and forth (just like with the real models I saw on television) because of my bouncy mattress. I even had a plastic tiara which said Princess on it and was given to me as a birthday present. Back then, I was *totally* a model and a princess all in one.

The sound of her spoon connecting with the sides of her mug while she stirred brought me back to reality. "No, I haven't," I said with what I hoped sounded like conviction.

The woman threw her head back and laughed again very loudly as a server approached us. "Would you like anything else?"

We declined and she brought over some water.

It occurred to me that this woman, who hadn't even properly introduced herself yet — heck I hadn't given her my name either — was trying to woo me into going back and purchasing the dress. It had to be about the dress. "I'm still not buying that dress," I said rather abruptly, "no matter how much you flatter me."

She threw back her head and I thought she was going to let rip with another roar of laughter but this time she did not. Instead, she leaned in closer to me, changing her mask to a profoundly serious one and said, "I think you handled yourself back there in a very classy way. You didn't lose your cool and I agree with you — the dress wasn't you." That got my attention. I leaned in.

"We at Goddess Creator Fashion don't want our customers to live in the past. We want women like you to buy clothing to suit their current needs." She took a sip of water, swallowed, cringed and continued, "I can tell you've lost some weight recently. A fair amount maybe?"

I beamed out a smile which told her everything she needed to know without having to utter a single word.

"So now you are a woman in transition. You want to lose more, and while you're losing you want to dress beautifully, to feel beautiful and that dress made you feel like the person you were before, now didn't it?"

Unexpectedly I reached across the table and shook her hand. She knew me and we'd only just met. I felt shy now, like she could read my mind, but also comfortable that she knew me. I was feeling quite pleased with myself and perhaps even a little over-confident.

"May I ask, why you tried it on in the first place? Why did you take it to the counter or consider buying it?"

I answered immediately, from the heart, "I was trying to make myself look better on the outside so that I would feel better on the inside — but it had the opposite effect." I put my hands over my face to cover up the blush.

"Open up," she said, "you're a beautiful girl whether you are Size 20 or 10. Now, will you consider trying out to be a model for Goddess Creator Fashion's new line? Will you think about it?" She handed me her business card, paid the bill. We shook hands. "Call me," she said, "but don't take too long."

"I'll call you," I said knowing perfectly well that I wouldn't.

"I expect to hear from you in one week. The ball is in your court — because I don't even know your name and I won't have any way to contact you. It's one hundred percent up to you," she said almost like she knew.

As she walked away, "thank you for your time," I said sounding like she was a store clerk. Duh. It sounded dumb as soon as I said it.

Her face changed, like I had slapped her but only for a second. Then she smiled a big smile and asked, "What is your name love?"

"Christina Langdon," I replied.

"Well, Christina Langdon, it was good to meet you and I hope you'll be in touch. We met today by chance. Some might call it fate. It is up to you if you want to take advantage of the situation. I hope you won't let this opportunity slip by. It would be Goddess Creator Fashion's loss. Bye now," she smiled, then turned and walked away.

After she left, I sat staring into space for a long time. When they closed up the Café, I was still there pretending to drink the same cup of water when I realized I should fill Brandon in on my news. I texted - *Goddess Creator Fashion wants ME to try out to be a model!*

To which my best friend for my entire life replied: "*WHO IS THIS?*"

By the time I read it, my phone was buzzing, and it was Brandon. "OMG!" Brandon said, "My very own best friend is going to be a Goddess Creator Fashion model!"

He sounded even more excited about it than I was, and that is exactly why Brandon Daley was my absolute best friend. We'd been friends before we were even born — our mothers were BFFs — and they hung out incessantly when they were carrying us in their wombs. We weren't related by blood, but we were related through friendship and love and it was an unbreakable bond.

"Earth to Christina," Brandon said. "Yoo-hoo! BFF!"

I'd drifted off in my imagination, not realizing he was waiting for me to fill him in on all the details. It had all happened so quickly. It almost sounded too absurd to say it, to talk about it out-loud.

"When you're finished work, I'll tell you all about it."

"Oh sure, keep me in suspense!" he said followed by, "Bitch!" with a laugh and then he disconnected.

Ah, the term of endearment of that five-letter word.

I smiled and decided to head to the gym. Exercise, surprisingly even to myself, had become like a religion to me. When I hit the gym, I could solve problems and think things through calmly and rationally. Nothing cleared the mind more than a decent work out.

CHAPTER THREE

O N THE WAY THERE, I resisted temptation by ignoring the nine fast-food joints en route. Getting to the gym was a little like having to run the gauntlet. I now had even more reason to keep slimming.

Did those fast-food joints have a strategy to catch people on the way to or from the gym? Did the real estate agents send out gym related demographics? I mean nine in a row, two blocks from the gym seemed like a master marketing plan to entice the easily tempted. It made sense, in a conspiracy theory way of thinking and if true was evil sabotage.

That's why, I always carried a protein bar in the glove box and a piece of fruit in my handbag. Those fast-food tycoon bastards were definitely not sabotaging this bitch.

Since I started working out regularly, I always kept a gym bag in my car along with a bottle of water. Just knowing I have everything ready to go at a moment's notice made it possible for me to lose the first twenty-five kilos. I still had another twenty-five to go but keeping ahead of the cravings made my day-to-day existence easier. I was like a warrior equipped for battle — organized, focused, and winning.

The first time I went to the gym, I got lucky. I was paired with a Fitness Trainer who would assess my fitness level and work out a plan all during the free introductory session. His name is Alex, and he is a couple of years older than me and is super-hot. Alex encouraged me and pushed me in a gentle enticing way. Giving up was not an option. It was Alex who suggested I have a gym bag at the ready at all times. I joined the same day and have never looked back.

Now, as a fully-fledged club member with a bona fide photo I.D., I had certain privileges.

I tried not to look smug, as I sauntered past the long queue of newbies (potential or soon to be club members.)

I swiped my card, took a step forward and my knee hit the gate which hadn't budged. I glanced back over my shoulder as I heard an exhale of air from one of the newbies.

I scanned my pass again, praying without moving my lips. Once again, nothing. This time I heard a low guffaw from the queue. The thing still didn't recognize me. After trying a couple more times, I had no choice but to face the queue and get to the back of the line since there was only one guy on duty.

Eventually though, with a little help the computer recognized my card and let me through. I'd get myself together and be out on the floor ready to sweat off the daily stresses (and a few kilos) in record time.

Once I hit the gym, the first stop for me was always the treadmill. I stayed on there for the longest amount of time, so it was good to get it out of the way and it seemed to energize me too.

If you're not a regular gym-goer or don't go to the gym very often, it is difficult to get used to the smells. Today, more than ever when I walked out onto the floor it hit me like a salute. You'll know what I mean if you've ever been to a gym yourself - I won't explain any further. For those of you who don't go to the gym, it's the pungent smell of sweat, blended with body odours, deodorants, colognes, and perfumes. Some folks overdo the latter in the hope of disguising the former.

Although it was pongy, it was an enjoyable time to be there, few posers (people who didn't need to be there just hanging around looking smug and annoying the hell out of the rest of us.) The air conditioning was blowing like a Canadian winter and it was making me sweat with chills. I needed to start working out and the sooner the better so my nose could become blind to the smells and get myself warm. I was beginning to regret the too fast consumption of the in-car Protein Bar because it hadn't done much to help with my low blood sugar level.

Now at my favourite treadmill (I never used others, this was my treadmill and if it wasn't vacant, I changed my exercise routine.) I placed my water bottle in the slot, draped my towel over the side and set my paperback novel down. It was a vampire novel, lots of hot bits. The perfect distraction so I didn't look at the time or calories burned or any of that stuff until I was finished.

After a horrific experience reading Hemingway on the treadmill, I tried to keep my reading material light. On that particular day when I first started exercising, I had placed *For Whom The Bell Tolls* onto the dashboard of the treadmill. I started walking at a steady pace on Level two of ten.

Hemingway's writing has always made me forget about everything else in the world except for his book, and this time was no different. I totally forgot I was walking on a moving platform and the result was not good. You see, my book was resting on the dashboard of the thing — you know the place with all the control buttons? So, when I turned the pages unknowingly, I was touching the button below, increasing the treadmill speed and changing levels.

It went up slowly, gradually. I was doing fine, keeping up, that is until it hit 8.5. I'm not sure really what happened. All I know is, I let out a blood-curdling scream and everyone turned to look at me.

The look on their faces, of pure panic was one I will never forget. I was quite a sight with my Hemingway clenched in one hand, while my other hand was desperately jabbing the button to slow the damn thing down. No matter what I did, it continued picking up speed.

Panicked and stupid — I know a really bad combo — I hit the RED BUTTON, yes, it was the Emergency Stop button. Whoever called it that, got it exactly right because I violently lurched to a full stop. After that I banned Hemingway from coming to the gym with me. Wouldn't you have done the same? Hemingway, a firm believer in exercise himself, definitely would have forgiven me for the ban.

Everything went smoothly on the good old treadmill today. The vampires kept me distracted just enough and after I had wiped down the equipment with a towel, I made my way on over to the rowing machine.

The rowing machine was where I did all of my serious thinking since I couldn't read, and audio books weren't my thing. I sat down betwixt two burly fatherly types.

When I first started learning to use the rowing machine, I could only manage five minutes tops, but now, I could row for twenty minutes straight and pick up speed as I went. I strapped my feet in. Set the timer. Pulled the reins back and started rowing. I envisioned rowing somewhere exotic, like The Grand Canal in Venice.

Speaking of went, *they were soon off;* I mean the two guys on either side of me.

I could row alone in peace and think this entire modeling idea through. Or so I thought.

As I got into the groove rowing, imagining the water before me, I remembered the first time I ever tried aqua aerobics. I was at my biggest size then and getting into a bathing suit was not a decision I took lightly. However, most of me would be under the water, hidden once I got in, so I somewhat reluctantly agreed to give it a go.

Getting to the pool, I wore a floaty multi-coloured robe over my one-piece bathing suit. I sat on the edge, dropped it, and took the plunge. The water was beautiful, surprisingly warm and with only my head and shoulders on view, I waited patiently with the other girls for our teacher to arrive.

Gazing around at the competition, I was the only participant under the fifty-five mark. Yes, I was a water aerobics virgin. No worries though I thought. Boy did I get that wrong.

When our instructor arrived, a drop-dead gorgeous man with wind swept blond hair, a head-to-toe tan, and a physique like no other man I'd seen in the flesh, the other ladies cooed and catcalled. I felt a blush running up my cheeks at their forwardness. His name was Theo, and he took it all in stride. He was clearly used to being the centre of attention.

I continued rowing, trying to get my thoughts back to the modeling offer, but memories of Theo would not allow me to.

Now back in the pool in memory, we were asked to go and grab a water "noodle" ––i.e., one of those polyethylene foam jobbies the kids use. Theo then instructed us to ride said noodle like it was a horse. Before long, I was laughing so much I wasn't getting much done. Some ladies looked in my direction and rolled their eyes which made me laugh all the more. In fact, so much that I stood out enough to attract Theo's attention and he winked in my direction. I swooned and tried to pull myself together.

We handed in the noodles, grabbed some water weights. It was amazing how light they were under water. The other ladies were lifting twice as much weight as me and doing the lifts quicker and easier. Showoffs. I struggled to keep up, as the sun beat down on us and hoped Theo would call time soon.

After that, it was like a high school sports team pick with me being the last one chosen. We ran a relay race and our team won. The prize for the winning team, a sugar free popsicle. The prize for the runner's up also a sugar free popsicle. As winners we had first dibs on flavour choice.

The next day, I was so sore I couldn't even get out of bed. Every single part of me, even my hair hurt like hell. That's when I decided to switch my routine indoors and discovered I loved rowing.

I needed to focus on Goddess Creator Fashion. Theo, I wonder what ever happened to him? Goddess blast it, focus Christina. Will I or won't I?

One of the guys rowing beside me finished and left. It was at that moment Vanessa Pringle made her grand entrance. She was a size 0 and even though she and I had attended the same High School together for four years, I swear I never saw her take a single bite of food. Ironic she had the same name as my favourite potato chips. Even when she was in the cafeteria, she never ordered anything besides bottled water. She'd put it onto a tray and then bully the weightier kids about what they had on theirs. I hated her and felt sorry for her at the same time. I was convinced she was an anorexic. She must've had a pretty sorry life to make others feel so bad.

She came right over to the rowing machine and glanced in my direction, seeing me rowing at a good pace. She made like she was going to row right there beside me. In my heart of hearts, I knew I could kick her ass on this thing if she'd just let me. I looked in her direction, always the people pleaser. I even attempted to say hello.

Our eyes met briefly and then she totally dissed me and went on her merry way in the direction of the posers. She fit right in there, in front of the mirror with the others who liked to admire themselves while they flexed and primped during their work out.

Once she was gone, I wanted to think about the modeling offer. Now I really had to focus.

I was going along nicely, as the guys beside me came and went. Two more guys sat on either side of me. Fatherly types. On my left, he was in his sixties (give or take a few years) and on my right, in his forties (maybe late thirties.) Both of them started up slow but moved into a steady pace in no time.

I began counting. It always helped me focus since I was a little girl. As I counted up, I began to increase my speed and soon, I was rowing so quickly the guys on either side of me had trouble keeping up.

I tried not to gloat, while at the same time I tried to come up with a single definitive reason I should turn down the offer by Goddess Creator Fashion to be a model.

At first, my mind went blank. There weren't any reasons to turn the offer down. However, I had some doubts about my lack of experience. I was certain they would have a boot camp or some kind of training. The CEO knew I didn't have any modeling experience and still she had made the offer.

The other thing, the most important thing holding me back was plain and simple fear. Was I too chicken, too afraid to put myself out there? Would I, could I be an inspiration, or would I just be a target for other bitches like Vanessa?

As I examined these feelings of inadequacy and fear, it hit me. Since they were looking for a Plus Size Model for their new line — why should it be anyone else? Why couldn't it be me? Nothing ventured, nothing gained right? Funny how clichés always came in handy when trying to convince oneself to do or not to do something.

The two guys had left their machines without me even noticing until the timer went off on mine. I came to a stop, unhooked myself and looked around while I caught my breath. I took a sip of water.

At this stage, I was about eighty percent certain I would try out for the modeling job. Gathering my things together, I went over to the mat to do some stretches. I lifted a few weights using the exercise ball for support, then headed over to the stationary bike.

Vanessa approached the biking area from the other side and waited for me to choose a bike, then sat down next to me.

I busied myself, setting everything in motion. I started to put my headphones on when Vanessa said something. "Sorry. I didn't hear you."

"Oh my," she said, "this is very embarrassing. I so wasn't talking to you. I wouldn't want to distract you from losing all of that," — she pointed at and poked the girth around my waist. Who did she think I was, the Pillsbury Dough Boy?

I pushed her hand away, put my headphones on and went back to pedaling and reading. She was so rude, but I wasn't going to stoop to her level. Within seconds, a gaggle of girls swooped upon the area where they decided to have a raucous conversation.

No matter how much I turned the music up — and I was getting volume warnings — the tunes were drowned-out by their jocularity.

"And then he said..."

"And then she said..."

"And then..."

In unison, "Ohhhhhh!"

I looked around, to see if any of the trainers were noticing the guffaw. Usually, they would have stepped in by now and told the gaggle to fly the coop. No such luck today.

I hoped if I ignored them, they would just go away, but fifteen minutes later they were still as loud as before. I powered down the bike and decided to head home.

"Don't go away mad," Vanessa said, "just GO AWAY!"

How original, I thought as I made my way across the floor fighting the urge to flip the bird at her. I was just about to enter the change room when I saw my personal trainer Alex clocking on.

"Is everything all right Christina?" he asked as he touched me on my forearm.

Vanessa's flock stopped talking, eyes glued on Alex and me. "Yes, I'm fine," I said, as I beamed a big smile "but I wonder if I could talk to you for a second in private?" I said the "in private" part rather more loudly than normal — and I checked to make sure they heard.

"Sure, come on into my office and have a seat."

We went in and he closed the door. He sat down at his desk, put his hands behind his head, leaned back. "What can I do for you?"

His stomach, his flat abdominal muscles, his firm arms. To be honest, I couldn't answer his question. The palms of my hands had gone all sweaty. Especially when I imagined him climbing over the desk and planting the biggest most passionate kiss on my lips. I gulped in some air and could feel my cheeks becoming extremely hot. So hot, that he noticed and offered me a drink of water.

I took a deep breath and told him all about the modeling offer.

He jumped up and I closed my eyes in anticipation of a kiss. I felt so silly when I opened them, and he was standing there looking at me. It was awkward, but he threw his arms around me. He smelled good.

When we broke from the embrace, he smiled. "Of all my trainees, you have worked the hardest. You've put in the time. Even when you wanted to give up, you didn't. I'm proud of you. I believe that everything up to this point was preparing you for this offer."

I felt totally verklempt, like I was going to cry. "Thank you."

I left his office wobbling like a pool of jelly. Besides Alex, red jelly was what I was craving, red strawberry Jell-O with a big mound of whip cream on top. Thank goodness I had an apple in my bag, and I drooled all the way home thinking about Alex's abs.

CHAPTER FOUR

B EFORE YOU FIND OUT for yourself, I might as well fess up. I am twenty-two years old and I still live at home with my mother and older brother.

When I arrived home, Mom was cooking up her usual feast. I went over to give her a big hug and to look into the pot to see what was cooking. Mom was and is an excellent cook, and as a family we had been trying to work together and eat more healthily. We eat lots of veggies, some protein and we always have some fruit for dessert. It wasn't always this way though. Before we were enablers. We used to do a lot of stress eating. Since we started working together as a family, we've been able to keep each other on the straight and narrow plus we'd become closer.

"How was your day?" she asked, as she stirred away at the spaghetti sauce.

I kissed her on the cheek and told her about my workout. She had already guessed where I had been as my makeup was smudgy and my hair was still a little more than damp. "Did you get yourself a new frock?" she asked. "Go and fetch it and model it for me."

Mom was always like that. It was like she had a sixth sense about any kind of news concerning my brother or me. I smiled then tried not to gloat, but I couldn't help myself.

"You look like the cat who swallowed Tweety Bird. What's up?"

When I didn't answer straightaway, she came over to me and pressed her lips to my forehead like she had done a zillion times since I was a little girl with an elevated temperature. We didn't need a thermometer in our house because her lips told the tale with one hundred percent accuracy.

"It was the plan Mom to buy a dress, but it didn't work out today."

The spaghetti sauce furiously bubbled in the background piping up because she had been neglecting it. It spat at her as she gave it a quick stir.

"There's always tomorrow," she said. "You can find something then. Where did you go, to Goddess Creator Fashion? You always find something you like there."

"It's where I went, I tried on a dress. It was pretty and all, but something about it just didn't feel right. Even though I'd lost some weight, it still made me look fat."

Mom continued stirring the pot, thinking carefully before she answered, "your body has changed, but your mind hasn't caught up yet — is that it?"

Mom always floored me with her perceptiveness. Like many times before, she had hit the nail on the head. Maybe she just had that Mom ESP thing going on. Osmosis or something like it. Then it occurred to me — if I didn't tell her and super quick, she might actually guess about the modeling thing. No way, it was too far-fetched. And yet, she had asked me to model the dress. Did she have a gut feeling or was it just a coincidence?

She continued, "I've been on this planet for sixty years and as you know I've gone up and down in my weight like a Yo-Yo."

Mom went to the refrigerator and grabbed a bunch of spinach, washed it under the tap, spun the leaves dry in the salad spinner and then tossed them into the sauce.

Mom was a plus size goddess herself and she raised me to be one too. As I watched her move around the kitchen, tending to the thing she loved the most — cooking — her beauty radiated.

I remembered the times at school when I was bullied for being overweight and Mom told me how she too was bullied when she was a teenager. People could be so nasty, so cruel. If I put myself out there as a plus size model, what was this going to do to her, to our lives? Would it be like telling everyone in the world that we were proud of being over-weight? Fat shaming was the nation's favourite pastime.

Mom came to me and gave me a big hug while I was lost in thought. We sat down together, shared two Fig Newtons and a cup of coffee.

Content now, I wanted to tell her, but it still felt weird to say the words out loud.

"Mom, the CEO of Goddess Creator Fashion has asked me to try out to be one of their models."

CHAPTER FIVE

I 'M NOT SURE IF stunned is the right word I should use to explain the look on my mother's face but stunned is for certain what she was. In fact, for the first time in my entire life, my mother was speechless.

"Mom, are you all right?"

Her quietness was disheartening. I could almost see the wheels spinning in her mind. Was that smoke coming out of her ears?

She let out a little giggle, stifled it, then giggled again. She proceeded to walk over to the sauce. stirring vigorously while it snapped, popped, and spat a blotch onto her apron.

"I'm not kidding mom," I touched her hand to stop the stirring and looked her straight in the eyes. "I'm not. Really."

She hugged me like a hurricane forgetting she had the spoon in her hands and threw sauce all over the kitchen walls and ceiling and me. Now that she had taken in my news, she was so excited and yet she still could not speak.

Her silence was very odd. Mom was rarely silent, not when her kids had news to share, especially happy news like this. It affected me, because it brought back all the feelings of self-doubt, I had worked so hard to overcome and put out of my mind at the gym.

I tried to consider things from her perspective. Was she worried the woman was playing me? Pulling my leg? I had been gullible before but not about anything as important as this. I had been mistreated. Bullied, because I was naïve, believing people were friends when they were not. Maybe she thought I couldn't do it.

If she didn't think I could do it, then I had to find the strength within. This I knew, still, I wanted to run and close the door and never come out. have a strong tendency for over-dramatics — I apologize in advance.

I fell down hard into a kitchen chair, stuffed another Fig Newton in my mouth and waited for my mother to tell me what she was thinking. The packet of biscuits was half full or was it half empty? I could wait her out with these distractions.

CHAPTER SIX

I WAITED, WAITED, AND then I ate another Fig Newton.

Mom picked up the packet, closed it and walked over to the cookie jar. She took off the lid.

I took the CEO's business card out of my handbag and placed on the table beside me. I crossed the room and put the card on the table beside where mom was closing the cookie jar.

I sat back down again. I watched her pick up the business card. She looked at it for a second, then went back to the sauce.

"Mom?"

"What exactly did this woman say to you?"

"She asked if I had ever thought of being a model."

"And have you? I mean have you ever thought about it?"

I could feel my face turning red. Mom didn't know about my bed runway, about me wearing her high heels and jewelry.

"I have thought about it," I admitted, "but it was a long time ago when I was a little girl."

"All little girls play dress-up," mom offered.

"But they all aren't invited to try out to be a model for Goddess Creator Fashion – now are they? And not by just anyone. The Owner and CEO of the company invited ME. Personally. She saw something in me."

Saying those words aloud, made me feel defensive and cross.

Suddenly I was more than a hundred percent certain the offer was for me.

CHAPTER SEVEN

I COULD TELL MOM wanted to think about what I had said. Pretending to have an urgent message, I left the kitchen.

Once I sat down, I put Mrs. Sharon Lindt's details into my phone. I felt so angry at Mom's strange reaction. First, she hugged me and seemed so excited that she threw sauce around the room and then she went all zombie-ish. To spite her, I nearly called Mrs. Lindt and accepted her offer without delay.

While I was waiting for Mom to come to her senses, for some reason I kept thinking about my dad. We hadn't seen him since I was a little girl. Mom never spoke of him and we never knew what happened to him. One day he was here and the next, gone. I thought about all the times, when he would sit on the floor with me and play doll's house.

We'd come up with all kinds of fantastic ideas to get Barbie and Ken active in the world. Traveling to London, Paris, Rome and even to Sydney, Australia. When he first went, I missed him very much but now, after he left us without a word, not even a simple goodbye, well, I hardly missed him at all.

Mom came into the living room, wiping her hands on her apron. I realized it had been a long time since I really looked at her. I mean really looked at her. Here I was, telling her about this fantastic thing happening in my life, and what did she have to look forward to? Since Dad left, her life turned into one hundred percent just caring for my brother and me.

Mom never treated herself or bought herself anything pretty although she encouraged us to do so. She had been with my dad for nearly fifteen years when he left. Did she think of him? Did she miss him? Was she lonely? Mom told me that she would one hundred percent support whatever I wanted to do with my life as long as I was certain it was what I wanted. She continued, "modeling is a dog-eat-dog business and in order to make it, you'll have to work your butt off. Even if you were asked to model for Goddess Creator Fashion, it doesn't mean it is the right career choice for you."

"It is a risk, but one worth taking. What's the worst thing that can happen? I fall flat on my face in those heels?" We both laughed at the thought of me sprawling across the runway. "Well, I wouldn't be the first or the last — I think it's worth giving the modeling world a try. I hate my job at the Call Centre. I want more for myself, don't you think I deserve a shot at something different? Something better?"

"You'll be your biggest obstacle and critic Christina. Sure, there will be other critics in the world, but you have to remember no matter what they say, you only have to please yourself. You don't have to live up to their expectations."

She was right, if I let them shine the spotlight on me, I had to be strong enough to both accept and deflect what was said about me. Inner strength would be key. Without it, I would be adrift in the world of skinny binny models, trying to fit in. "I want to make a difference, for all the girls out there like you and me who never had a chance. I want to show them beauty comes in all shapes and sizes."

"I think you've got it. Now why don't you give that lady a ring and then let's sit down and have some dinner?"

"I might just sleep on it," I said.

Mom looked at me with concern, then acquiesced. She returned to the kitchen and I could hear her out there, washing and keeping herself busy. I knew she was trying to send vibes out to me to make the call now before I changed my mind, but the what ifs had begun to seep in.

I saw mother return to look in on me, just as my phone began to hum.

The caller I.D. revealed it was Sharon Lindt, Goddess Creator Fashion.

"Here we go!"

CHAPTER EIGHT

S HE RECOGNIZED MY VOICE straightaway. We chatted briefly. Mrs. Lindt said she had found my contact details online. "I wondered if you had any questions for me now you've had the chance to mull things over a bit? I do hope you have been seriously considering my offer."

"Yes, Mrs. Lindt, it's all I have been thinking about. I'm interested in finding out more about your proposal. What is it exactly I would need to do? As I told you before, I don't have any modeling experience."

She sounded pleased, really pleased. "First things first, call me Sharon. No experience necessary. For the right candidate, we will train. Also, I forgot to tell you about the incentive, for trying out. That's why I thought I'd give you a call this evening, so you have all the details and can make an informed decision."

"An incentive for trying out?" I grinned. Mom moved closer, to listen to my phone with me. Instead, I put Mrs. Lindt onto speakerphone so Mom could hear everything said live too.

"Yes. In addition to training, the winner will receive an All-Expenses Paid trip to the Goddess Creator Fashion Show in Paris. We've been laying the groundwork; it is going to be one amazing opportunity for one young woman to participate in. Once she joins the Goddess Creator Fashion Team, the sky will be the limit."

I couldn't help myself, like a little girl I let out a squeal. So did Mom. I nearly fell off my chair. I had no idea there were fashion shows in Paris for larger women, but why shouldn't there be?

Sharon must've been able to detect this in my voice because she continued with, "we are getting a lot of attention for the show. If you're chosen, we'd love it for you to be a part of it. It's not easy, but whoever we choose, Goddess Creator Fashion will be one hundred percent behind them."

"It would be a dream come true, to go to Paris," I cooed as my mind rambled on to thoughts of climbing the Eiffel Tower and strutting along a runway. Of eating French pastries, drinking the real thing Champagne, visiting the Louvre,

Jim Morrison's grave and dancing along the Champs-Elysees.

"Are you still there?" Sharon asked.

"Yes, I'm just a little star struck. I don't have a passport, and I can't speak French fluently."

Sharon laughed. "That's perfectly fine. You'll have time to get everything sorted — after the Boot Camp if you're chosen. We have people on board who can help if need be. Don't worry about details. Just worry about saying yes and winning."

The words Boot Camp echoed in my head. I envisioned what it would be like. A room filled with full figured girls, made up to the hilt, tucking themselves into stylish clothes and wrestling with their high heels for the prize, a once in a lifetime all-expenses paid trip to Paris. I wanted it. I wanted to win.

"One more thing. If you win, you can bring along a family member to Paris to see your Debut on the défilés de mode — translated that means Fashion Parade."

Mom let out a scream I'm certain was heard all the way to France.

"Yes," we both said together into the phone.

"I'll put you in touch with a few of my staff members. They'll fill you in on the details for the Boot Camp. It'll allow you the opportunity to get used to the idea, to dip your toe into the water a bit at a time rather than submerging your entire foot in all at once."

"That sounds absolutely wonderful," I said. I was so excited I could hardly speak properly, and I was hanging onto my phone with an iron grip.

"One more thing," Sharon said, "Casser une jambe. It means break a leg in French and I mean it. I'm with you Christina Langdon. Best of luck."

Mom and I nearly fell over in excitement.

"Oui! Oui!" we sang into the phone.

CHAPTER NINE

Today is Boot Camp Day! Here I am rummaging through my closet, making a huge mess and still without a single thing to wear.

"Knock, Knock," Brandon said, and as always, he came in before I had the time to tell him to.

"OMFG Christina, you need to, you know, just put something the fuck on so I can take you to Boot Camp — you don't want to be late."

He moved over to the bed, picked up a pair of black pants with leather stripes along the outer pant leg and a button up blouse — "you'll need a black bra for this," he chided and off I went to change. Brandon had the most wonderful sense of fashion, especially for women. I wondered if one day, he might be a famous fashion designer himself but no, he was happy to work with me and the others at the call centre every single day.

I put myself together and it wasn't long before I was dressed and ready to go, I was so excited my hands trembled when he said in a tres annoyed tone of voice, "Uh, makeup?"

"What would I do without you?" I asked as I sat down in front of the mirror and began applying it. "Not too much," Brandon chided.

In the meantime, he sat behind me, brushed my hair, and then tied it up. "So, they can appreciate your swan-like neck." I giggled.

I put on some flats and we made our way downstairs, where Mom was waiting, smiling like a parent sending her child off to Prom Night.

Mom gushed, "You look so beautiful!" She didn't often gush, and it made me feel even more excited as she snapped a few photos and promised not to post them on social media without my approval or Brandon's. On the way out, I hugged her, and I could tell she was fighting back the tears.

My knees buckled as we made our way out to Brandon's hatchback. To calm our nerves, we stopped for lattes via the drive through. Although we were running a bit late, we knew there was always time for a coffee break.

"Butterflies are going crazy in my stomach," I admitted.

"OMG! I'm having empathy butterflies!" Brandon cooed.

We laughed like crazy. Until one of our favourite songs, by The Doors came on the radio. Brandon cranked it up full blast and we sang at the top of our lungs. Before we knew it, we arrived in the parking lot where Boot Camp would soon be happening.

Brandon got out of the car first. I couldn't budge. He came around and opened the door for me and said, "You've got this bitch."

I laughed, smoothed down the front of my outfit and stepped out. Together we made our way to the entryway.

The building was grey with silver trim on the outside, but it had lots of windows. It looked like it used to be a factory, in a good sort of way. We sauntered through the revolving doors, holding hands. Brandon was always there to give me moral support — he was my rock.

The entryway was grand, with a lot of gold trim along the edges of escalators and glass chandeliers in all shapes and sizes hanging from the ceiling. We oohed and ahh'd as we made our way over to the security desk.

"Christina?" the man in the uniform asked.

"Yes, it is I." WTF? Where had that come from? Pretentious or what?

Brandon laughed and shoved me forward.

I wasn't doing it on purpose, it was all down to nerves. "How did you know my name?"

"Come around and have a look," Travis Whiting (the security guard) said to me. When I went through the gate, I saw a photo of myself on the computer. It was one taken from my Facebook profile or from somewhere on the net. Not the most flattering photo but at least he recognized me.

"Cool," I said, but then I looked up and noticed Brandon was standing on the other side of the turn style, "He's with me," I said.

"I'm sorry, no one is allowed beyond this point without pre-approved entry or a security pass," Travis said.

Brandon looked very dejected, but he understood it was out of my control "I'll go and troll the neighborhood and see what's happening. Text me when you need me, and I'll come back to collect you. Have a wonderful time at Boot Camp! Knock'em dead!"

I blew him a kiss and watched as he went around the revolving doors waving, once, twice then three times. He blew me a kiss and mouthed the words, "Three times lucky."

I blew another kiss back.

Travis gave me directions to Boot Camp. I took a deep breath, checked my makeup in a mirror en route and off I went.

CHAPTER TEN

A T THE END OF the long hallway, filled with shots of gorgeous women of all shapes and sizes were two large windowless doors. I point out the windowless part because from the outside this place had plenty of windows. But we were way in the back, deep within the heart of the building. It meant I couldn't look inside the Boot Camp room beforehand to suss out the place nor was anyone else.

Excited I walked by all the other girls. They stared at me. A couple nodded. I pulled on the handle to go in and get myself settled and nothing happened. I tried the other side of the double door entryway and again nothing happened.

"Uh," a girl just behind me said, "we have to wait here until they let us in."

"Oh, thank you." I paced a bit while singing in my head some Tom Petty lyrics about waiting.

"Your first time?" the same girl asked.

I nodded just as bells began to ring rather loudly. At first, they were slow rings, then they rang faster and louder. All the girls stood up and moved forward, trying to pivot into a good spot. Magically the doors opened, and we surged forward. I felt like Dorothy entering The Land of Oz.

We stuck together at the entry way at first, then as a group pushed inwards and soon arrived in the centre of the room for a moment and I looked around. There were exceptionally long wooden seating rows on the left and the same long seating rows on the right. The thought of sitting down was at the forefront of my mind. I was so nervous. Excitement and anticipation filled the air with electricity as we waited.

Over the loudspeaker, a woman's voice announced, "Welcome to Goddess Creator Fashion candidates. Please line up in a single file starting with the tallest to the shortest. Thank you."

We did as she asked; I was midway down the line.

"Starting with the tallest, please take a seat on the left on one of the seating arrangements. Once all the spots have been taken, the rest of the candidates please take seats accordingly on the right-hand side benches. Please remain seated and you may talk quietly among yourselves for a few moments. Loud voices and/or aggressive behavior will result in the removal and/or lifetime ban of contributing candidates. We at Goddess Creator

Fashion thank you for coming and wish you all the best of luck!"

Now seated, we were looking across the room at each other. Sizing each other up. No matter what, we were all in a competition together. Fighting for the right to earn a spot. The women there were all exceptionally beautiful, some noticeably young and some around the same age as me. A few were older, more experienced and their sense of fashion screamed pick me. True, we had one thing in common in that we were all Plus Sized, but some were on the cusp due to having height to their advantage.

I was thinking about where I fit in and what my chances were when a tall girl on the other side caught my attention. She was a true stunner and oozed confidence. She smiled and mouthed, "good luck," and I did the same back to her. It was nice of her to do so, maybe this gig wasn't going to be, so dog eat dog after all?

The girl sitting directly beside me was shaking like a leaf when she asked, "Is this your first time? I'm Lilith, and you are?"

"Nice to meet you Lilith, I'm Christina and yes, this is my first time. I'm really nervous."

"Nice to meet you, I'm nervous too. This is quite intimidating – I mean when those big doors open up for the first time, but you'll get used to it and mostly folks who come here are nice once things get moving. They'll narrow the numbers down and if we make the cut, we get to stay and move on to the next stage."

"So, this isn't your first time then?" I asked.

"No, I've been here lots of times, but it always makes me so nervous," Lilith said. "For me, no matter how many times I come here, it's always like the first time."

I thought about coming here repeatedly and being rejected. It took a lot of guts to keep coming back. I said so and added, "So, they cut the numbers down?"

"Yes, pretty much straight away so they can get down to business," she said as she shivered. I noticed she had goosebumps running all along her forearms. I had been nervous, but now seeing how nervous Lilith was, somehow made me less nervous.

"No one told you about the process. Which organization recruited you?" she asked.

I didn't feel comfortable in telling her that the owner of Goddess Creator Fashion had recruited me personally. Instead, I said that a friend of a friend had connected me, and she seemed perfectly fine with that explanation.

"Once a month, they invite us here — give us a showing — but they usually only select a handful of girls to try for the next level. I've been coming here for six months now and so far they haven't chosen me to go beyond this the first level."

I quickly counted how many girls were there on both sides, including myself I counted twenty-five. Considering this was my first time, I figured the odds were not in my favour. In fact, I probably had little to no chance looking at my competition.

"What modeling have you done before?" she asked.

I lied again, "just local stuff, here and there. How about you?"

"I have my own website and I've modeled for Wal-Mart, Target, Sears and a few other chains when they were expanding their Plus Size fashion lines. I take any work I can get, but Goddess Creator Fashion, to work with them is my dream. I just keep taking other jobs, to add them to my resume in hope of one day making my dream come true."

"Wow, that's amazing," I said just as a woman dressed from head to toe in a hot red pantsuit made her way across the floor carrying a long pointy stick. Her spikey heels which looked to be at least five inches or so high made pucketa pucketa sounds as she crossed the room on the hardwood floors. The woman appeared to be at least 6 ft. tall shoeless, consequently she looked like a fricking skinny giant. Behind her, a man who was around 4 ft. 5 inches tall, followed tapping continuously on his iPad.

"She's really something," Lilith said, "just watch. I mean watch and learn."

"Scary."

"You ain't seen nothing yet."

I figured the woman would go along one side and then along the next. But no, she was going to intimidate first, then choose people randomly. Before she did though, she was going to walk around and look at us like we were puppies waiting to be adopted.

As she drew near to us, Lilith sat up straight and I did the same. Unfortunately, as I did so my phone fell out of my pocket and hit the floor. The woman didn't react or look directly at me (thank God!) as I retrieved it and dropped it into my handbag. I felt like such a newbie.

"Lilith Martin," the woman said, and I applauded.

Before she stood up Lilith whispered to me, "if she calls your name you're done." She took a deep breath, I could tell she was fighting back the tears, "Good luck and I hope to see you next time. I'm not giving up."

We shook hands briefly and then off she went. I felt so bad. Why had she knocked out poor Lilith and first too? No one wanted to be the first one to go. It was like being the first person voted off Survivor.

She called out name after name. I jumped when she spoke. Her voice was high pitched and with a register like nails on a chalkboard. All choices were random and for no particular rhyme nor reason that I could see. Soon there were only two left, the tall Amazonian candidate from across the way and me. This had to be some kind of joke. right? Me against her? I looked around, wondering if there were hidden cameras and someone was going to run out and yell April Fool's. Mind you we were nowhere near April.

"Come along," the woman said. The other model and I smiled as we made our way across the floor. The little man with the iPad took our photos as we came together and then continued merrily tapping away.

"Congratulations candidates," the woman in the pantsuit and her minion said in unison. She tapped her stick and turned.

"Thank you," we said.

"Let's get busy. We have work to do!" the woman said as she walked hurriedly across the room with the young man following closely behind.

We model wannabes brought up the rear.

CHAPTER ELEVEN

P LAYING FOLLOW THE LEADER we exited the hall. Soon we were in a separate room with a catwalk at the ready. The platform didn't seem as high nor if I had imagined it to be. The ones in the movies and on fashion programs always looked so high up and long. Maybe they made it lower so we newbies wouldn't sue them for injuries when we fell off.

"Let's get straight to it," the woman in the pantsuit said. "I'm Madame Levesque and you may call me Madame Levesque. This is my P.A. Jeremy Bolt."

We nodded hello and then she continued, "Jeremy will escort you to the change rooms where an assistant will choose an outfit and dress you both. You must wear whatever they choose for you including the shoes. They will then send you to makeup, where you will receive a full makeover.

Please listen carefully to all tips which the stylists offer you as they will be invaluable and without them you are nothing," she said like she'd said it a hundred times before all the while tapping her stick in time with each syllable.

My competitor put up her hand, like she was in class at school. Madame Levesque noticed but ignored her and began to walk away. How rude, I thought, but was sure glad I hadn't tried to ask anything.

This was all extremely exciting. I trembled at the thought of stepping out onto the catwalk and making my way down it. In my mind, I remembered on *Sex in The City* when Carrie Bradshaw had taken a fall. I laughed quietly to myself, as we continued following closely behind Madame Levesque.

I focused on having a full makeover. I felt so lucky to be given this opportunity.

We stopped and Madame Levesque tapped her stick on the floor twice.

"At precisely 2:15 p.m. you will be ready to walk the catwalk." She tossed a coin in the air, "call it," she said, and I said "tails." The coin hit the floor and rolled. Together we walked over to see the results, it was tails — I would have to go first.

"When the music begins, you will be ready. One after the other. You will walk down that catwalk — you will walk for your life. After I will decide which one of you will continue training at Boot Camp in preparation for our Goddess Creator Fashion Show in Paris. Good luck to both of you!"

My head was spinning as we followed Jeremy to meet our makers (or rather our makeovers.) It was a one-time opportunity and I simply had to be sensational.

CHAPTER TWELVE

M Y COMPETITOR AND I were separated without being formally introduced. She looked like a pro and being a newbie perhaps it was better this way. After all, without meeting me, she wouldn't have any knowledge of my lack of professional modeling experience. Since her name had never been called, nor mine we were both in the same boat.

When we arrived at my designated room, Jeremy opened the door with a flourish and kind of gently pushed me into the room and closed the door. I heard his footsteps outside as he walked away. Meanwhile, I stood there waiting for someone to acknowledge my presence — no one did.

"Yoo-hoo," I said. I imagined Carson Kressley was behind door number one. I went over, opened it but no one was there. I'd take any help at all. Even from those two women who had their own show on British television a few years ago. Nothing. No one was here. I was totally on my own.

I looked at my watch, realizing in precisely one hour I would need to walk down that Catwalk — and that walk would either make or break my career as a model.

I considered sitting down, but decided moping wasn't going to help my situation. I opened the door hoping to ask Jeremy for guidance, but he was nowhere in sight. I didn't want to panic and yet, I did. Not totally, but I rang Brandon and told him what happened, and he told me to get on with it — to get busy and to kick their asses.

After a few moments of sheer panic, I did what any red-blooded wanna be model would do, I started pulling outfits off the clothes rack. Narrowing down outfits. Hoping to save time when my helper arrived. Searching for the perfect outfit.

I took shots of items and sent them to Brandon, we narrowed it down and with my BFF's help I was well on the way to looking the part.

After several tries, and with the clock ticking and Brandon on speakerphone — we decided on a formal look, sexy but not too sexy. We chose shoes, handbag, earrings, and a tiny barrette for my hair.

"You don't think I'm cheating, do you?" I asked Brandon.

"Hell no," he said, "They didn't keep their end of the bargain. But you should hang up now love if you're all calm and ready. Practice makes perfect. Love you!"

"Love you too Brandon and thanks."

Now that I was dressed, I practiced walking up and down pretending I was on the catwalk. The shoes I had chosen were comfortable and I had no fear of falling or tripping. Now feeling super confident, I went to a mirror and refreshed my makeup and glanced at my watch. It was 2:10 and only five minutes left to show time. I quickly used the facilities.

With only moments to spare I fell into a comfy chair (careful not to wrinkle anything) and feeling very satisfied at what Brandon and I had accomplished. Together we were a regular tour de force.

A moment later there was a knock on the door, and it was Jeremy.

"No one showed up, to help me."

"I know." He glanced at my outfit and smiled. "Follow me."

"Wait. Why didn't anyone help me?" I asked.

Jeremy stopped, turned to look at me. "It's not my place to explain, but I can tell you one thing, you didn't need the help. You simply look fan-ta-bu-lous!"

"Thank you," I said, "Now let's get this show on the road."

Jeremy laughed.

Although we had walked down the corridor before, when we went back, we took another route and it seemed to take ages and ages to get there. I spotted my competition, with a team of people mostly women primping her hair and doing last minute adjustments. She looked stunning and she was ready and eager to go even though I was going to go first. She looked at me from head to toe and then looked away.

I got ya bitch, I thought.

I put my chin up and when the cue came, I walked out into the bright lights.

CHAPTER THIRTEEN

A T FIRST, I COULDN'T see anything because the bright lights blinded me. I remembered fashion shows I'd seen on television. Most models wore sunglasses but up until now I thought they were an accessory. Now I realized they were a much more important asset to have. I sure wished I had some.

In addition to being extremely bright, the heat pouring off the lights made me feel like my makeup was sliding and soon would be dripping down my face. I walked faster. Focused. Confident

I kept on walking. When I got to the end, I did a turn, with a flourish. I stopped, did a second turn, and made my walk back. When I reached the curtain at the end, I felt triumphant. I didn't fall. I had done it!

My competitor now had sunglasses on as she hit the catwalk. She was extremely comfortable out there, and even I could feel the excitement in the air as she did her thing. What she was wearing suited her, she had gone one hundred percent casual with jeans, a jacket, and a little cap. She had high-heeled boots on, spikey heels, and she did the turns perfectly and soon returned.

It was all over very quickly. Between the two of us, our walk for life had only taken minutes.

We stood side-by-side and waited in silence content in the knowledge we had done everything we possibly could.

CHAPTER FOURTEEN

A FEW MOMENTS LATER, Jeremy came out of nowhere. In his hands he held two white envelopes, one for each of us. After he delivered them, he turned tail and left. The Amazonian girl without hesitation tore her envelope open. I watched her face. Her expression did not change. She picked up her things and left. How strange.

All alone now, I put the envelope down. I took off my shoes and hit the catwalk. It might be my last chance to walk on it. This time, at the end, instead of turning around, I sat with my legs swinging off the edge. I felt like a little girl all over again. I wished Mom could have been here. To see.

Earlier, when the spotlights were on, I couldn't see much of the hall. Now, they were dim, and I could see there were no seats along the sides like I had expected there to be. The hall was pretty much an empty space. In some ways it was a sad space, too quiet. It longed to be filled with people and music.

Ready now, I looked at the envelope. I picked it up and tore it open. Inside were two airline ticket vouchers to Paris, hotel reservations, a credit card, some cash, and a handwritten note:

Congratulations Christina &

Welcome to the Goddess Creator Fashion Team!

I knew you could do it!

Sharon Lindt

President & CEO

Goddess Creator Fashions.

I fell back onto the catwalk, looked up at the ceiling, and cried like a baby. I couldn't believe it. I, Christina Langdon, was going to be a Goddess Creator Fashion model.

After calming myself down, I dialed Brandon's number. I sobbed out my location and told him to please come and get me. He said he would. I waited. I was so proud of myself. I couldn't wait to tell him my news.

"Babe, Babe," Brandon cooed when he came into the room. Trailing on his heels was the security guard who was red-faced and very cross. I hadn't thought about the guard. It hadn't occurred to me that my request would cause a scene. Meanwhile, Brandon rushed toward me.

Me, with my makeup streaking down my cheeks. Me looking like I had lost the role — not won it. He had the wrong end of the stick. I had to set him straight and fast.

"Those bastards! Those complete and utter bastards."

I burst into tears and then began to giggle. "It's okay."

Brandon must've thought I had finally lost it, because the look he got on his face went from empathy to anger. "Where are they?" he shouted. "Let me get at them, I'll, I'll..."

"Excuse me," Jeremy said. "What is all the shouting about in here? We could hear you all the way down the hall and Madame Levesque is not amused."

Jeremy had a quick word with the security guard, confirming he would manage the situation and the guard eventually left.

Meanwhile, I made a move to go to speak with Jeremy, but Brandon was too fast, and he pushed right by me. My BFF walked up to Jeremy and he did something

I could not believe he would ever do — he poked him. Yes, he poked him right on the chest and he said, "How dare you?"

Jeremy took a step toward Brandon and said, "HOW dare you!"

I ran over and pushed myself in between them. I put my left arm around Jeremy's neck and my right arm around Brandon's neck and I said, "I think we have a bit of a misunderstanding here."

Both boys were glaring at each other and it was like they could see right through me. Which is something considering my size and weight.

"Will you two please stop it and let me explain?"

It took a while, but they cooled down. I decided my best strategy was to divide and conquer.

"First of all, Jeremy,"

"And why is HE first?" Brandon interrupted with both hands on his hips. "Who is he anyway? You've known me for years. I'm hurt to the core. We are BFFs and now you're putting this stranger first? Over me?"

"Oh brother," Jeremy said.

Brandon took a step toward him, his face as red as a beat.

"Take a chill pill," I said.

He calmed down and I continued speaking to Jeremy and explained what had caused the misunderstanding. He laughed, all the while looking at Brandon. I could see it in his eyes, he admired how Brandon protected me. He smiled, then apologized to Brandon. They shook hands, agreed to let bygones be bygones and then Jeremy left the room. On the way out, I saw him look back over his shoulder. He was totally checking out

Brandon. Yes, it was just for a moment. I noticed but Brandon was totally oblivious because he was one hundred percent focused on me and my wellbeing.

I realized Brandon and Jeremy would totally make a really cute couple.

Now alone with Brandon, who was pacing like there was no tomorrow, I told him I got the modeling job and would soon be leaving for Paris. We danced around the room holding hands like two young kids. He was so happy for me and I was so happy for me. We'd done it together. Without his help, it would never have happened. We were totally even more BFFs.

Isn't life funny when you achieve a dream that you didn't even know you wanted? True this was only the beginning and I had a lot of work to do before I would be a true to life model, but the door was open now and all I had to do was work hard and I had a chance to make it.

We went out to celebrate, drank a few too many Mojitos. I teased Brandon about Jeremy, asking if he thought he was cute.

"Uh, I didn't even notice the guy with the iPad," Brandon said.

"Liar, and he was totally into you. He checked you out and everything."

"You're making it up," Brandon said.

"We'll see, but you two would make a very cute couple."

After getting home quite late Brandon crashed on the floor of my room overnight. In the morning, I told my mom and my brother the good news. Mom jumped up in the air and hooted. The four of us held hands and danced around in a circle. Everyone was so happy; we danced around like drunken Mexican jumping beans and had the most wonderful time.

"What are you going to take to Paris?" Brandon asked.

"What are you going to wear in Paris?" Mom asked.

"How are they going to understand you?" my brother asked.

"What are you going to do about your job?" they said in unison.

Too hung over to even think about any of their questions, I went back to bed and dreamed of Paris and Champagne! Like Scarlett O'Hara in *Gone with The Wind*, I was going to think about it in the morning.

THANK YOU

Just a quick note of thanks to you for reading, and to all those who helped me to make my book better including my editor(s), proof reader(s) and beta readers.

As always, Happy Reading!
Cathy

ABOUT THE AUTHOR

Multi-award winning author Cathy McGough
lives and writes in Ontario, Canada,
with her husband, son, their two cats and one dog.
If you'd like to contact Cathy please send her an
email to:
cathy@cathymcgough.com.
She loves to hear from her readers.

ALSO BY

FICTION
Thirteen Short Stories
Everyone's Child
Ribby's Secret
Interviews With Legendary Writers
From Beyond (2ND PLACE BEST
LITERARY REFERENCE 2016 METAMORPH
PUBLISHING)
Three Friends Wait 4 The 1

SHORT STORIES
The Umbrella and the Wind
Margaret's Revelation
Dandelion Wine (READERS' FAVOURITE BOOK
AWARD FINALIST)
Darryl and Me
The Brightest Star
Death Wish
NON-FICTION

103 Fundraising Ideas For Parent Volunteers With Schools and Teams (3RD PLACE BEST REFERENCE 2016 METAMORPH PUBLISHING)

POETRY

Painting With Words

YA BOOKS

E-Z Dickens Superhero Book One; Tattoo Angel.
Book Two: The Three,
Book Three: Red Room. Book Four: On Ice
E-Z Dickens Superhero Complete Series
A Mathematical State of Grace Complete Series

CHILDREN'S BOOKS

The Three Boulders
Billy Shakespeare/Billie Shakespeare
Jump Series
Clap Series